W9-BYG-075

EYE ON
ART

Computer Animation
Telling Stories with Digital Art

By Tanya Dellaccio

Portions of this book originally appeared in *Computer Animation* by Hal Marcovitz.

LUCENT
PRESS

Published in 2018 by
Lucent Press, an Imprint of Greenhaven Publishing, LLC
353 3rd Avenue
Suite 255
New York, NY 10010

Designer: Seth Hughes
Editor: Vanessa Oswald

Cataloging-in-Publication Data

Names: Dellaccio, Tanya.
Title: Computer animation: telling stories with digital art / Tanya Dellaccio.
Description: New York : Lucent Press, 2018. | Series: Eye on art | Includes index.
Identifiers: ISBN 9781534560970 (library bound) | ISBN 9781534560987 (ebook)
Subjects: LCSH: Computer animation–Juvenile literature. | Computer graphics–Juvenile literature.
Classification: LCC TR897.7 D39 2018 | DDC 006.6'96'023–dc23

Printed in the United States of America

CPSIA compliance information: Batch #BS17KL: For further information contact Greenhaven Publishing LLC, New York, New York at 1-844-317-7404.

Please visit our website, www.greenhavenpublishing.com. For a free color catalog of all our high-quality books, call toll free 1-844-317-7404 or fax 1-844-317-7405.

Contents

Foreword

When many people think of art, the first things that come to mind may be paintings, drawings, sculptures, or even pictures created entirely with a computer. However, people have been applying artistic elements to almost every aspect of life for thousands of years. Human beings love beautiful things, and they seek beauty in unlikely places. Buildings, clothes, furniture, and many other things we use every day can all have an artistic aspect to them.

Attempts to define art have frequently fallen short. Merriam-Webster defines art as "something that is created with imagination and skill and that is beautiful or that expresses important ideas or feelings." However, almost no one refers to the dictionary definition when attempting to decide whether or not something can be considered art. They rely on their intuition, which leaves much room for debate between competing opinions. What one person views as beautiful, another may see as ugly. An idea that an artist feels it is important to express may hit home with some people and be dismissed by others. Some people believe that art should always be beautiful, while others feel that art should be unsettling enough to pull people out of their comfort zone. With all of these contradictory views, it is no wonder that the question of what is art is so often disputed.

This series aims to introduce readers to some of the more unconventional and controversial art forms, such as anime, fashion design, and graffiti.

Debate on these topics has often been heated, with some people firmly declaring that they are art and others declaring just as firmly that they are not. Each book in the series discusses the history of a particular art form, the ways it is created, and the reasons why it is considered artistic. Learning more about these topics helps young adults recognize the art that is all around them as well as form their own opinions about this complex subject.

Quotes by experts in various art fields enhance the engaging text. All quotes are cited so readers can trace them back to their original source, giving them a starting point for further research. A list of recommended books and websites also allows young adults to delve deeper into related subjects. Full-color photographs give vivid examples of the artistic works being described in the books so readers can visualize the terms they are learning.

Through this series, young adults gain a better understanding of a variety of popular art forms. They also develop a deeper appreciation for the artistry that is inherent in the things they see and use every day.

The Beginning of Animation

The technological advancements of the last century have led to significant progressions in computer animation. The earliest animations consisted of simple drawings pieced together to form a sequence. Today, however, animators can transform a simple drawing or idea into a captivating, lifelike finished product. Animations are now created across a wide spectrum of stylistic choices, using both new and old technology. Classic illustrated techniques can still be seen in films, TV shows, and video games, as well as advanced computer animations with realistic settings and characters. The work required to achieve either of these outcomes is a long process and includes the time and talents of many artists and engineers. Requiring both art and science to bring an animation to life, artists and engineers, along with a long list of creative and technologically skilled staff, work together to create a finished product.

The first animators practiced their craft through a process referred to as cel animation. This consisted of creating thousands of individual drawings on clear sheets that flowed together to form a sequence of scenes that in turn were strung together to create a time-lapsed story. Each cel drawing was photographed and subsequently fed quickly through a projector to show the movements of both the character and the background. This tedious process was the beginning of storytelling through film animation. Several well-known movies were created through this process. In 1937, Disney released the first fully animated movie, *Snow White and the Seven Dwarfs*. The cost for production of this film was $1.5 million. It quickly grossed $8 million after its release, revealing the possibilities of what film animation could achieve.

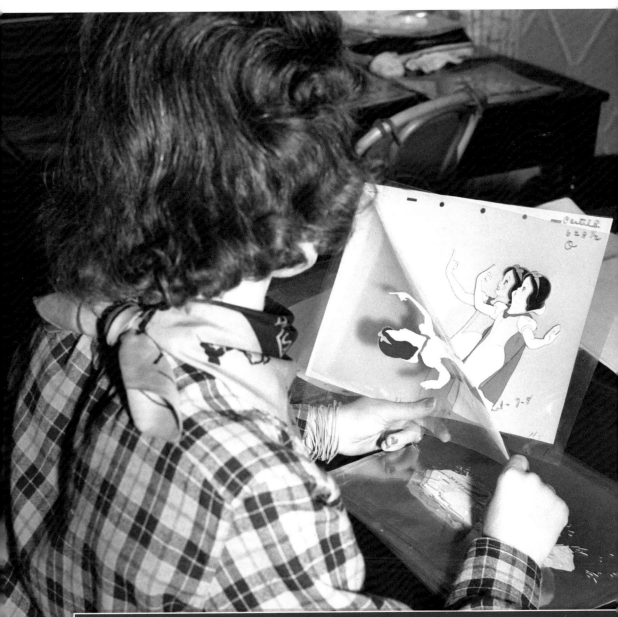

The film **Snow White and the Seven Dwarfs** *was created using cel animation. Each scene was composed of several layers of drawings laid on top of each other.*

Though this film was an unprecedented achievement at the time, it may seem outdated in comparison to today's computer animation. Even so, the past technique of cel animation gives the film an artistic style that cannot be compared to the modern computer-generated form because they are so different.

In the days of cel animation, the technology used for today's computer animation would have been unimaginable. These new techniques helped animators render three-dimensional forms and scenes, creating a more lifelike result. Computer-animated films are popular, though they remain distinguishable as cartoon-like animations. However, computer-generated images have opened up a new realm of possibilities, fusing computer-animated scenes and characters with real actors and sets. Today, viewers are able to watch films that are generated with such skill that what elements are real versus animated often remains unclear. This fusion is used cohesively in many aspects of visual entertainment today, and advancements continue to progress and open more doors for improvements and new possibilities in computer animation technology.

The first full-length film generated entirely with computer animation techniques was released in 1995. This film, *Toy Story*, wowed audiences and critics and

Toy Story *was the first fully animated feature-length film to be produced on computers.*

created a platform for the creation of many more animated films to come. Two of the largest animation companies, Pixar and Disney, created the masterpiece as a team. Steve Jobs, CEO of Pixar at the time, told *Fortune* magazine in September 1995, "If *Toy Story* is a modest hit—say $75 million at the box office—we'll both break even."[1] The film grossed approximately $361 million, a profit unimaginable before its release. After the film's extraordinary success, animators and executives at Disney and Pixar realized the magnitude of what computer animation could achieve. Multiple *Toy Story* sequels have been produced, and each new release has earned a profit significantly higher than the last.

The early pioneers of animation could not have imagined the advancements that computer animation has allowed for today and, with these advancements, the possibilities for both entertainment and everyday life that computer animation could and would provide. The average person is surrounded by images stemming from the history of animation—whether a film, a game, or advertisements—and computer animation has opened up an entirely new way of looking at things.

CHAPTER ONE

Progression of Techniques

Though today the world of computer animation is advanced, its beginnings can be traced back to several simple concepts that eventually progressed into the science of computer animation. Early forms of animation were created with little to no technology and were primarily executed by hand. These early practices provided a solid foundation for the advancement of animation. There were early attempts at motion pictures long before cel animation was able to capture images in motion. In some of the earliest cave paintings, there are progressions of scenes drawn out in order, representing a lapse of time and hinting toward a range of motion throughout a storyline.

Another early attempt at images in motion was the *thaumatrope*. This device was primarily a toy for children; however, the underlying concept was much more advanced. A card, often circular, had two images drawn on either side, with two pieces of string at each end. As the string was twisted between two fingers, the two images, moving quickly around and around, appeared to merge together. One of the most common examples of a *thaumatrope* is one in which the two images are a bird and a cage. As the string is twirled, the bird appears to be trapped in the cage. This example is similar to that of a flipbook, wherein several

images are drawn in progression on individual pages in a booklet. When flipping through the booklet quickly, the succession of images moves across the page, simulating motion. Often flipbooks tell quick stories, such as that of a man tripping or the life cycle of a flower. Both examples, stemming from the 18th century, give us an insight into the earliest attempts at animation. Though basic in comparison to today's technology, these examples of movement through images were incredibly groundbreaking in their time.

Furthering these practices, early glimpses of animation began to occur. Starting in the early 1900s, people

Though not as advanced as computer animation, experiments such as the thaumatrope, *shown here, led to the development of moving images.*

began telling stories through moving images. These early stories were drawn by hand and, though advanced for the time, were simple by contemporary standards. Since then, animation has progressed to a point where it is sometimes unrecognizable whether an image or character is real or animated. Thanks to some of the top pioneers of animation and the successful studios that followed them, computer animation is a part of almost every film and is present in many other aspects of life as well.

Cel Animation

As previously stated, prior to advancements in computer technology, most animated features were produced through cel animation. The cels were transparent sheets of paper, onto which each illustration was drawn. For years, the sheets were made from cellulose. Today, however, cels are made from the synthetic substance acetate. Creating a film through cel animation is an incredibly lengthy task. Even for the briefest features, thousands of cel drawings are created. Each scene for the film is illustrated onto a single cel. Scenes are often created in layers, with a bottom layer containing the background illustrations and several transparent sheets placed on top containing different stylistic elements and illustrations of the story. Most animators would shoot 1 cel per frame of film and then film the cartoon at a speed of 24 frames per second. Therefore, a 5-minute cartoon would require 7,200 cel drawings; for a 90-minute full-length feature film, artists produced nearly 130,000 cels.

In 1908, a French director, Émile Cohl, composed a brief animation titled *Fantasmagorie*. This piece is considered to be the first example of an animated cartoon. The film, which featured the social interaction between a clown and a man, was produced using just 700 simple black-and-white line drawings. In 1911, American newspaper cartoonist Winsor McCay developed a two-minute animated film titled *Little Nemo*, which featured various storylines from the dreams of a young boy named Nemo. McCay drew each image for each frame of film himself. *Little Nemo* was a much more detailed animation in comparison to Cohl's *Fantasmagorie*. McCay began to understand the potential for animation and created several more successful short films throughout his lifetime.

One of the most notable early animators and the one who has been given the most credit for developing the craft of animation is Walt Disney. He produced the cartoon *Steamboat Willie* in 1928. The animated feature introduces the character Mickey Mouse as he navigates a steamboat over a river. It was an immediate hit among audiences. Animation historian Charles Solomon wrote, "Disney managed to book it into the Colony Theatre in New York for two weeks. *Steamboat Willie* premiered on November 18, 1928. The cartoon was a smash hit."[2] The film was produced in black and white, employing many techniques that print cartoonists had been using for years.

Steamboat Willie established Disney's studio, known by 1929 as Walt Disney Productions, as the preeminent animation studio of its day, and the studio has maintained that status for nearly a century, becoming one of the industry's top innovators. Mickey Mouse, first introduced in this short film, remains one of the world's most popular animated characters.

By the early 1930s, animators were employing simple colors in their

Today, archives of many early cels are stored in climate-controlled libraries. Shown here is a cel setup of Rocky from the 1960s cartoon Rocky and His Friends.

features. Disney produced the first multicolor Mickey Mouse cartoon, *The Band Concert*, in 1935, followed by the first feature-length animated film, *Snow White and the Seven Dwarfs*, in 1937.

Stop-Motion Success

Stop-motion animation can be seen in a number of successful films today. One example is the movie *Coraline*, which was produced by the stop-motion animation studio Laika. *Coraline* was released in February 2009 and grossed more than $16 million in the United States during its first weekend alone. This film follows a girl named Coraline and her eerie adventures into an alternate world. The production team used props and characters modeled from clay for each sequence, which means that each moment was composed of thousands of different images. Since each clay prop was shifted around several different times, multiples of each small detail were constructed. The set even had a clothing designer who made hundreds of tiny "costumes" for each character. Three years later, the same team at Laika produced another movie, *ParaNorman*, also using the stop-motion technique, which grossed more than $14 million in the United States during its opening weekend. Though many refinements have been made to the practice since the early 1900s, the look and feel of a stop-motion film is something that cannot be reproduced through average animation techniques.

Stop-motion films require time and patience to complete. Each movement is filmed shot by shot in order to achieve the proper progression of the film.

Early Efforts and Whirlwind

Through the efforts of Disney and many other creative people, cel animation became the standard for the industry, but other artists were also experimenting with alternative animation techniques. Starting in the early 1900s, many artists were drawn to the technique of stop-motion animation, which employs the use of puppets made out of clay or a similar malleable substance. The puppets are photographed repeatedly as they move throughout a scene. As with cel animation, 24 frames are shot per second, which means the animator must move each puppet at least 24 times to produce 1 second of film. If there are two or three puppets in the scene and each puppet is using its mouth, hands, and feet, there could be tens of thousands of manipulations required to produce a film that runs a few minutes. Stop-motion animation proved to be a highly sophisticated form of art, and it continues to be used in films today. In the 1920s and 1930s, stop-motion animators were put to work by major Hollywood studios to produce images for some of the most popular movies of all time, including *King Kong* in 1933.

Following World War II, television exploded as an entertainment medium in the United States and elsewhere, and animators responded by providing programming for the new television networks. By the 1950s, animated cartoons such as *Crusader Rabbit*, *The Heckle and Jeckle Show*, and *The Woody Woodpecker Show*, as well as the stop-motion show *Gumby*, had arrived on television. While television became increasingly popular and more accessible, university computer laboratories were experimenting with different technological advancements that would eventually have a dramatic impact on the entertainment world.

Starting in the 1930s, at a time when audiences were awestruck by the animation of *Snow White and the Seven Dwarfs* and the stop-motion effects of *King Kong*, computers were first starting to come into use. One of the first computers, Harvard University's Mark I, was 50 feet (15.25 m) long, weighed 5 tons (4.5 mt) and took as long as 12 seconds to compute the simplest mathematical problem.

During World War II, computer technology made a great leap forward with the development of the University of Pennsylvania's Electronic Numerical Integrator and Computer (ENIAC), which was able to perform 100,000 calculations per second. ENIAC weighed 30 tons (27 mt) and required so much electricity that it occasionally dimmed the lights throughout the city of Philadelphia, Pennsylvania. ENIAC was developed with the help of funding from the United States military, which hoped to use the computer's data to pinpoint targets for artillery gunners.

The war ended before the computer was finished. Nevertheless, the government liked what it had seen, and over the next few years, many computer-science research projects were funded by the military.

In 1951, a project at the Massachusetts Institute of Technology (MIT) known as Whirlwind produced a rudimentary flight simulator for the United States Navy. At the time, computers did not feature screens, but the MIT engineers were able to transfer the data to the screen of an oscilloscope, which could display simple graphics. Oscilloscopes had been used for many years to display impulses of electrical current produced by industrial equipment and similar devices. The image on the Whirlwind screen depicted the eastern coast of Massachusetts, while a symbol moved over the coast, simulating a flying aircraft. A major development in the project was the light pen stylus. When the light pen was pointed at the simulated aircraft, Whirlwind produced text on the screen that identified the plane as well as its speed and direction. This was the first example of being able to "click" to receive and move data on a computer screen.

Animation Pioneers

Scientists working at other university laboratories developed similar projects. In 1956, scientists at the University of Michigan were able to simulate the movements of military vehicles. In 1958, MIT scientists working under a United States Air Force contract developed a technique to print computer-generated pictures. Meanwhile, corporations started exploring computer imaging as well. In 1959, engineers at General Motors produced computer-generated drawings that were displayed on ordinary 35mm film. A year later, a scientist at Boeing Aircraft, William Fetter, coined the term "computer graphics" to describe the work he had been doing in designing the cockpits of airplanes.

By this time, computers were starting to employ screens to display text as well as graphics. In 1960, the Digital Equipment Company, one of the first computer manufacturers in the world, introduced the first computer equipped with a monitor—the Program Data Processor-1. It sold for $120,000. The Digital Equipment Company also equipped the device with a keyboard.

Meanwhile, other innovators developed techniques that would prove to be important to computerized filmmaking. In 1960, filmmaker John Whitney Sr. adapted a computer-driven device that armed an antiaircraft gun with a camera; using high-contrast photographic film, Whitney was able to produce abstract art. Whitney gained most of his knowledge of computers by taking them apart and putting them back together. In doing so, he was able to create moving structures on the computer screen. This talent landed him a job with one of the first computer technology companies, IBM. With access to more sophisticated computers such as those at IBM, he was able to create more sophisticated animations, which generally showed the constant movement of several complicated geometric figures.

In 1964, Ohio State University art professor Charles Csuri found himself awestruck by an image printed in a publication produced by the school's electrical engineering department. The image showed the profile of a female face. It had been produced on a rudimentary printer that resembled a typewriter. By using just a few letters of the alphabet, the programmer was able to fabricate the image and color it in shades of gray. "When I saw that first picture," Csuri recalled, "I could not believe what I was looking at. I saw the implications, and it hit me like a bolt of lightning. I immediately enrolled in a computer programming course."[3]

In those days, before the widespread use of keyboards, most data was entered into a computer through punch cards, which consisted of small cardboard cards with holes placed in various points. The holes in the cards were read by the computer, which produced information based on what the punch cards instructed it to do. Once he learned the basics of programming, Csuri generated printouts of drawings by inputting tens of thousands of punch cards into the Ohio State computer. In fact, Csuri was able to instruct the computer to simulate paintings by such renowned artists as Pablo Picasso, Paul Klee, and Francisco Goya.

In 1967, Csuri programmed the computer to produce a short animated film titled *Hummingbird*. The computer generated 30,000 images, which were then transferred to movie film. The movie, which showed a rendering of a hummingbird in flight, was the first true computer-generated animation. A year after Csuri produced the film, it was obtained by the Museum of Modern Art in New York City, where it has remained a part of the museum's permanent collection. After producing *Hummingbird*, Csuri continued to experiment with computer graphics.

A student studying computers from MIT, Ivan Sutherland, stumbled upon an idea for his doctoral dissertation that changed the world of computer animation. In 1961, what came to be titled Sketchpad was created. This was the first multi-functional drawing software for computers. Through this program a person was able to draw an image on a tablet with a light pen. This image would show up on the computer screen and from there they were able to make either the whole part, or a certain section, move. A more advanced, updated version of Sketchpad is still available today. However, many other companies have created alternative software that is more advanced and better suited for the process of computer animation.

Computer-Generated Imagery

Viewers of *Hummingbird* might have laughed at the notion that computers could ever replace animation produced by the human hand. The art in Csuri's film is simple; *Hummingbird* was rendered entirely in black line drawings on a white background. The film is also brief, lasting just 10 minutes, and there is no story—it simply shows the motions of the bird in flight. As Csuri screened *Hummingbird* for audiences on the Ohio State campus, Disney's hit cel-animated movie *The Jungle Book* debuted in theaters. The cel animation for *The Jungle Book* provided vibrant colors and plenty of action. The film also included the voices of big-name stars, hit songs, and a plot the audience could easily follow. On television at this same time, the popular Marvel Comics superhero Spider-Man was animated into a weekly show. The cel-animated *Spider-Man* proved to be a hit and was renewed by the ABC television network for two more seasons.

However, there was interest in the entertainment community to push computer animation into new and creative directions. At first, most of this interest was among producers of television commercials. Television commercials then generally concluded with an image of the sponsor's logo. These were the first computer-generated images that started appearing in commercials during the 1970s. Movement in logo design was just the beginning. Today, a large percentage of commercials have some aspects, if not all, generated by computer animation.

Elsewhere in the entertainment industry, great strides were being made in using the computer to enhance special effects on film. Filmmakers began using their knowledge of animation to produce computer-generated imagery, more commonly referred to as CGI. Computer animation generally refers to 3-D forms and characters constructed completely on the computer, whereas CGI is the practice of fusing together real scenes and characters with computer-generated aspects that enhance the film.

The first film to employ CGI was *Westworld*, which was released in 1973. *Westworld* tells the story of a futuristic amusement park where guests can play the parts of Wild West characters. Some of the characters in this film are portrayed as robots. *Westworld* features scenes from the robots' points of view. To show the audience what the robot is seeing, the image was scrambled by the computer, which resulted in a pixilated version of the actual scene. In 1977, a much more advanced film featuring CGI was released. The title of the film was *Star Wars: A New Hope*.

Star Wars: A New Hope made cinematic history. The story of intergalactic rebels fighting against an evil empire generated a worldwide audience that was suddenly hungry for science-fiction adventures. It also set a high benchmark for CGI, featuring sophisticated scenes of animation that were produced by the computer.

By the late 1970s, the hardware and software needed to produce computer animation had developed far beyond the machinery and techniques that Csuri had used to produce *Hummingbird* just a decade before. By no means was *Star Wars: A New Hope* an animated film, however; it featured actors, life-sized props and sets, and live-action filming. The director, George Lucas, made wide use of miniatures and other well-established special-effects techniques.

However, Lucas did merge several computer-animated scenes into the final print of the film. For example, in the closing minutes of the film, the hero, Luke Skywalker, must navigate a jet fighter over the mechanical terrain of the Death Star on his way to shooting a kind of torpedo into the ship. The surface of the Death Star was computer generated. In the film, the terrain speeds by under Skywalker. It took the computer animators a month to produce 2 minutes of footage, and just 40 seconds were used in the final cut of the film. The last four seconds of

The technology used to create the computer-generated imagery for the Death Star in 1977's Star Wars: A New Hope was a crucial advancement in the technology that made the use of computers in live-action films more accessible.

the sequence—the moment when the torpedo falls into the core of the Death Star—were drawn by hand. Still, there is no question that *Star Wars: A New Hope* revolutionized the use of CGI. The Star Wars franchise has gone on to include several prequels and sequels after the first successful film in 1977. Many spin-off television series, such as *Star Wars: The Clone Wars* and *Star Wars Rebels* have also been released. Disney went on to purchase George Lucas's company, Lucasfilm, in 2012. Though the buyout transferred all rights of the Star Wars franchise and Lucasfilm projects to Disney, Lucas's ideas and input on each Star Wars film is highly regarded.

The First Partnerships

In 1975, Lucas established his own special-effects company to develop the CGI for his films as well as other studios willing to pay for his services. He named the company Industrial Light and Magic. As Lucas worked on his sequel to *Star Wars: A New Hope*, titled *Star Wars: The Empire Strikes Back*, he created a new division of Industrial Light and Magic. This division would concentrate solely on developing techniques and equipment that filmmakers could use to produce CGI effects. The division, which he called the Graphics Group, developed some truly advanced research. Nonetheless, in 1986, Lucas decided to sell the division because it was losing money. Lucas opted to concentrate more on making movies

and less on developing research for other moviemakers.

He sold the Graphics Group for $5 million to Steve Jobs, one of the founders of Apple Computers. Jobs invested another $5 million of his own money and renamed the company Pixar.

Jobs was initially interested in developing hardware that could produce animated images, which he believed would have use in the defense and medical industries. However, one of the company's earliest customers turned out to be the Disney studio, which employed Pixar's hardware as well as software of its own development to produce images for its animated films. Disney was the first studio to use a computer to produce the images that cel artists had been doing for years. In 1989, Disney produced *The Little Mermaid* mostly through the "ink and paint" process; however, the final shot of the film, which depicts the wedding scene of Prince Eric and Ariel, was produced using a computer.

Pixar developed its own software and became an independent film production company, first making computer animation for television commercials and then expanding into feature films. In 1991, the Disney film *Beauty and the Beast* included sequences produced by Pixar's computers. Most of the film was produced through cel animation, but the backgrounds in the ballroom sequence—in which Belle first dances with the Beast—were rendered by computer animation. If the ballroom scene had been hand-painted by artists, it would have been a flat, two-dimensional rendering, and the characters would simply have danced across a static background. By using a computer, the filmmakers were able to add a three-dimensional perspective to the background, changing the viewpoint of the scenery as the two characters danced through it. As *Beauty and the Beast* producer Don Hahn recalled,

> *The ballroom sequence is the bonding moment of the film when the two main characters finally get together. For us filmmakers, the computer offered us a way to get heightened emotions on the screen and more dramatic effects than we could have gotten conventionally. It allowed us to move the camera around and take a look at the room instead of just looking at a flat piece of artwork. Technology as a whole is an extension of our fingers, hands, and minds. Computer graphics let us go beyond what we can currently achieve with pencil and paper or paint and a brush.*[4]

The dazzling computer animation included in the film helped *Beauty and the Beast* earn an Academy Award (also known as an Oscar) nomination for Best Picture in 1992 — making it the first animated film ever to receive an Oscar nomination in that category.

A year later, the Disney film *Aladdin* made even more use of computer animation. In the film, Pixar computers created the animated sequences inside the Cave of Wonders and also produced every image of the magic carpet that is featured in the film. It was the first time a complete character in a feature film was animated by the computer.

After the success of *Beauty and the Beast* and *Aladdin*, it became clear to executives at Pixar and Disney that a full-length feature film could be produced entirely on the computer. In 1995, Pixar and Disney partnered to produce *Toy Story*. The story presents the adventures of toys that come to life. The film features the voices of Tom Hanks as Woody, the toy cowboy, and Tim Allen as Buzz Lightyear, the toy space ranger.

After Hanks and Allen read the dialogue in a recording studio, some 300 technicians spent a total of 800,000 hours behind their computer screens, fashioning the artwork for the 81-minute movie. It took up to 15 hours of work to produce each frame of film. The work paid off; in *Toy Story*, audiences saw a breed of animation unfold on the screen that they had never seen before. That film's success helped launch an entirely new kind of feature-length filmmaking.

Beauty, The Beast, and CGI

A new *Beauty and the Beast* film was released in March 2017. The recreation of the film featured the same storyline, with an updated cast of computer-generated characters. Unlike the first film, where just the ballroom scene was produced through the computer, almost all the scenes in the remake included some sort of computer-generated material. Many of characters in the remake were almost entirely computer-generated, with the exception of a few, including the main character, Belle, played by Emma Watson. The Beast, however, was a mix between motion-capture technology and computer-generated material. The character was voiced and played by actor Dan Stevens, who acted out several scenes, which were then animated over onto the computer to portray the Beast. Since a real person played the part of Belle, making the Beast look realistically comparable was crucial to making this film a success. The divide between the live-action elements with the animated ones in this film needed to be seamless, allowing those "heightened emotions" to take place without questioning the authenticity of the characters.

Remaking films previously created with early animation techniques demonstrates the progression of computer animation, while also providing audiences with a more in-depth cinematic experience of a familiar storyline.

Top Studios

In 2006, Disney agreed to buy Pixar for more than $7 billion—showing how important the computer animation studio had become in the industry in the 20 years since Lucas agreed to sell the company to Jobs for $5 million. Since then, Pixar has gone on to produce some of the most profitable movies of all time. Though the companies sometime function as separate entities, more so Disney than Pixar, the Disney-Pixar collaboration is to thank for most of the top animated movies today, including *Finding Dory*.

Finding Dory was released in June 2016 and is ranked as having the highest-grossing animated movie debut in U.S. history as of 2017. Other popular titles created by Disney-Pixar include *Inside Out*, *Up*, *Cars*, and *Wall-E*. Disney, on the other hand, has independently created successful computer-animated movies such as *Zootopia*, *Frozen*, *Big Hero 6*, and *Moana*.

Today, Pixar faces competition from more than a dozen computer animation companies, some of which are underwritten by Hollywood's most important studios. One of Pixar's main competitors is the computer animation division of DreamWorks. The studio, founded by

Finding Dory was the most successful animated film of 2016, grossing more than $486 million in the United States.

director Steven Spielberg, has produced movies such as *Trolls* and *Shrek*, as well as the Netflix series *Trollhunters*. DreamWorks remains one of the most profitable animation companies, though it has had fewer top box office hits than Disney and Pixar.

Another studio with several notable computer-animated films is Universal Pictures. It was founded in 1912 and has produced many highly rated films, both animated and live action. The studio's most notable computer-animated films include *Despicable Me, Despicable Me 2, Minions,* and *The Secret Life of Pets.*

Other companies that provide CGI effects are also in high demand. Since animation has spanned not only to 3-D graphics in film, but also to animation in live-action movies, studios like Industrial Light and Magic are still a huge part of the animation industry. Though now overseen by Disney, Industrial Light and Magic has provided special effects for many top films such as those in the Star Wars, Jurassic Park, and Pirates of the Caribbean film franchises.

CHAPTER TWO

The Gaming Industry

As the technology that made computer animation possible progressed, so did the ideas for its use. People began experimenting with other uses for computers and, in turn, other uses for animation. One of the biggest alternatives to film animation is animation in video games. Progress in animation allowed artists and programmers to create animated games that could be altered and directed according to the moves and decisions of the player. What is now an industry that brings in billions of dollars a year started out just as film animation did—a simple concept that evolved into a more advanced product.

Today, there are video games where the characters on-screen look and move like real people, almost indistinguishable as animation. Technology has advanced far enough that virtual reality headsets are available that essentially block those wearing them from the outside world, allowing users to interact and play along solely with the alternate world in front of them. Science journalist Keith Ferrell stated, "Graphics, sound, motion: All must come together to create a believable illusion. The goal, some feel, is interactive fiction as striking in image and sound as motion pictures."[5] All of these believable illusions were made possible by the experiments and accomplishments of various early game designers and animation pioneers.

Spacewar!

One of the earliest games that sparked the gaming industry was created in 1961 by a group of students at MIT. They used the school's new Program Data Processor-1 (PDP-1) computer to develop a game they called *Spacewar!* The game featured the simplest of graphics—basically points of light on the screen—but players could maneuver a spaceship around a star while battling enemy ships. The PDP-1's manufacturer, the Digital Equipment Company, eventually received permission from the students to distribute the game along with the PDP-1. Therefore, anybody who had access to a PDP-1 could play *Spacewar!* Of course, since a PDP-1 computer cost $120,000, the game was played mostly in university laboratories, corporate computer departments, military installations, and other institutions that could afford expensive computer equipment. As such, it was not available in the consumer market. Still, during the 1960s, engineers and software designers continued to experiment

Spacewar! sparked the creativity of many game designers, leading to much more advanced versions of it, and thus began the history of the gaming industry.

with manipulating images on computer screens, knowing that eventually electronic games could be fashioned for home players.

Later, in 1966, a man by the name of Ralph Baer began creating what would be known as the first video game console—the Magnavox Odyssey. The gaming system was released in 1972. This console, which connected to a television set, featured 12 different games. All were variations of light movement on the screen and required different plastic overlays to be placed on the television screen for the view of the games to function properly. Games included sports such as hockey and football, as well as casino games such as roulette. Although it was the first at-home console that worked with a television, since it was marketed at $100 and could only be used with a Magnavox television set, it was unattainable by most consumers.

Nolan Bushnell and *Pong*

A frequent gamer, Nolan Bushnell, became inspired by the aspects of *Spacewar!* and the opportunities that both computer-based and television-based games could hold. He became interested in game development when he was a college student, often playing *Spacewar!* on the computers at the University of Utah, where he received an engineering degree in 1968. Bushnell went on to become one of the most notable pioneers in the development of video games. He became one of the founders of the electronic game industry when he developed *Pong* and later established Atari.

After graduating in 1968, Bushnell and his friend Ted Dabney adapted *Spacewar!* to play on an ordinary black-and-white television

Nolan Bushnell, shown here, was by far the most noted pioneer in the gaming industry. His creation of Pong *is an iconic part of video game history.*

set and renamed the game *Computer Space*. They developed a hardware console that hooked to the television. The console—a rudimentary computer—could do nothing more than play the game on the television. They formed a company named Syzygy to sell the game, but they were able to sell just a few models. Players found the instructions too difficult, and Syzygy was soon out of business.

Bushnell and Dabney learned a valuable lesson from the failure of *Computer Space*, and they resolved to develop a new game that would be more user-friendly. Bushnell recalled, "To be successful, I had to come up with a game people already knew how to play."[6] They each contributed $250 and started a new company, which they named Atari, which is the word for a maneuver in the Japanese board game *Igo*. The first game they developed was an electronic version of ping-pong, which they called *Pong*.

Instead of building new consoles for home sales, Bushnell and Dabney released *Pong* as an arcade game. They envisioned it standing next to pinball machines in bars, soda shops, and bowling alleys.

A *Pong* machine was nothing more than a blank screen that featured a white dot smacked back and forth by the players, who used knobs to control the two virtual paddles. There were even sound effects; when a player hit the "ball," the machine emitted a definitive "plink."

In 1972, the first *Pong* game was installed in a bar named Andy Capp's in San Jose, California. Bushnell and Dabney set up the *Pong* console next to a pinball machine. There was one line of instruction printed alongside the screen: "Avoid missing ball for high score."[7] By the second day, the machine had broken from overuse. Bushnell and Dabney returned to fix it. At the end of the first week, the *Pong* machine earned the inventors $300. The pinball machine standing nearby took in a mere $30 during the same period. Word soon spread throughout San Jose, and within days, the bar was jammed with young adults eager to play. Eventually Atari manufactured some 19,000 *Pong* machines, selling them mostly to bowling alleys and bars.

Developments occurred quickly. Atari grew into a major manufacturer of arcade games and soon entered the home-consumer market as well. The company developed a home version of *Pong* in 1975; it connected to a television set through a component that could easily be attached to the terminals for the television antenna.

In 1976, Bushnell sold Atari to Warner Communications for $28 million. A year later, Atari manufactured a home console, the Atari 2600, that accepted game cartridges. This was a tremendous step forward in game technology. Now a console did not have to be dedicated to a single game but could play a wide variety of games. Players controlled gameplay with a joystick, which took its name from the main steering device found in airplane cockpits. Using the joystick, players could start and stop the action, change the direction of their characters, and, if the game required it, fire a weapon by pushing a button on the stick or its base.

Among the games available for the Atari 2600 were *Pac-Man*, which called on players to send a hungry, circular character through a maze while he gobbled up points; *Space Invaders*, in which players fired missiles at descending lines of alien attackers; and *Breakout*, an advancement on *Pong* that required players to make bricks in a wall disappear by ricocheting a ball against them with a paddle. In the first year the Atari 2600 was on the market, the company sold approximately 250,000 of the machines at a price of about $200 each; by 1979, Atari was selling a million consoles a year.

Nintendo

Japanese artists and engineers designed some of the early games for the Atari 2600 and its competitors. One of those competitors was Nintendo, which was founded in the 1880s as a manufacturer of playing cards. In 1974, Nintendo obtained the rights to sell Ralph Baer's creation, the Magnavox Odyssey, in Japan.

The graphics produced by the Atari 2600, the Magnavox Odyssey, and the other early systems were miles ahead of the dots of white light found in *Spacewar!* By today's standards, though,

they would be considered simple. *Pac-Man* was, after all, just a yellow ball with a small opening for a mouth that continuously opened and closed. Still, there was a definite artistic component to designing each game. As technology progressed, the boundaries for that component opened up, sparking a flood of creativity that led game companies to experiment with a more detailed style of art for their gaming experiences.

Nintendo decided to develop a game featuring a more complex character of its own design. In 1977, the company handed the job to its staff artist, 24-year-old Shigeru Miyamoto, who was delighted to tackle the assignment. As an art student at the Kanazawa College of Industrial Arts and Crafts, Miyamoto loved playing arcade games and believed he could improve on the graphics found in *Space Invaders* and *Pac-Man*. Using the classic tale of *Beauty and the Beast* as inspiration, Miyamoto began to consider concepts for the new game. With the story as a reference, he created a storyline in which the player's task would be to rescue a princess from a villain, which was an ape. To save the princess, the player would have to leap over barrels and other obstacles the ape tossed in the way. Each time the hero jumped over a barrel, he scored points for the player.

Next, Miyamoto worked on the design of the main character—the hero whose movements would be controlled by the player. Working with the engineers at Nintendo, Miyamoto knew that their ability to adapt graphics to the game screen was still quite limited, so to stand out against the background of the scene, the character would need oversized features. He filled many notebooks with sketches and finally drew a short, stout man with a large nose and floppy moustache. Since the engineers advised Miyamoto against drawing long or bouncy hairstyles since they were difficult to animate, he drew the character wearing a bright red hat to avoid animation complications. This character was later called Mario.

To name the game, Miyamoto proposed to use the word Kong in the title because it suggested the image of an ape. He also flipped through a Japanese-English dictionary and found the word "donkey," which in Japanese means "stupid" or "goofy." Therefore, he had the name for the game: *Donkey Kong*. After production was completed, the game was shipped to the United States for distribution. Marketing teams were given the task of translating the instructions and game text to English, and with that, developing English names for the characters. The ape would still be named Donkey Kong. The princess, Pauline, was named after the wife of a Nintendo employee in the United States, and the main character of the game, Mario, was named after the company's disgruntled warehouse owner.

Donkey Kong proved to be enormously successful. The first 2,000 arcade machines sold quickly, and another 60,000 were soon shipped from Japan.

In its first 2 years, *Donkey Kong* earned Nintendo sales of more than $100 million. Soon after the game arrived in the United States, Nintendo licensed the title to Coleco, an American company, to produce a home version. In fact, many of the most popular games were being produced for home consoles to be played on televisions as well as personal computers, which were becoming more of a presence in American homes. Nintendo and the other game manufacturers found they could license the games to software companies, which adapted the titles so they could be played on home computers.

Today, Nintendo remains one of the leading video game companies. In 1990, it created the Game Boy. This gaming system was able to function alone, without the need for a television or computer. The portable console was created with a tiny screen and movement buttons below. A game cartridge was inserted into the back of the handheld console. This was a huge step in the gaming industry. In 1998, an updated version of the console was released that featured colored animation for the games. Today, much more advanced versions of these products are available. The Nintendo DS, first released in 2005, offered a flip-phone style with two screens—one for viewing the game playing and the other to make movements and choose options. A newer model, the Nintendo 3DS, features 3-D graphics and allows the player to maneuver through the game, playing the characters seamlessly through the portable console.

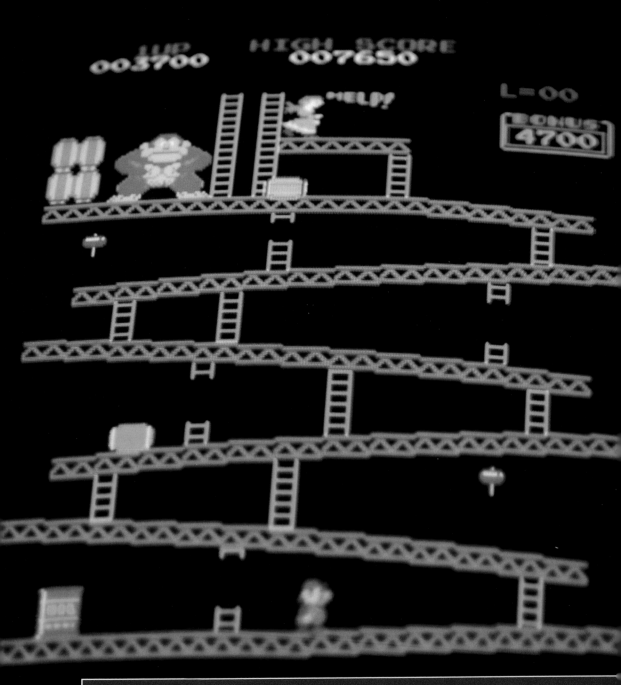

Several different games have been released with the characters from Donkey Kong. *Early animations of the characters, specifically* Donkey Kong, *have since been remade to reflect the updates in computer animation technology.*

Xbox

Several other consoles have dominated the world of gaming for many years. In 2001, Microsoft released the Xbox, a new gaming console that offered high-resolution images and a cleaner, more seamless way of playing. A year later, Xbox Live was released, allowing people to connect with other users through the Internet and play with them interactively through the gaming console. A new game was released with the Xbox that was specific to its console. The game *Halo* is a first-person shooter game where the player must accomplish missions and unlock different secrets as they go. The graphics of this game were a big step for CGI. Though they were still noticeably animated, the characters represented real people in a way that felt similar to live action.

Shown here is the first generation Xbox, released in 2001. A year later the digital media delivery service called Xbox Live was created.

Films Turn to Gaming Adaptations

By 1980, CGI had become a big part of Hollywood moviemaking. The sequel to *Star Wars: A New Hope*, *Star Wars: The Empire Strikes Back*, featured far more CGI shots than the original. Audiences were dazzled by the backgrounds surrounding Cloud City, which were created through computer animation. The filmmakers also used computers to animate the lightsabers wielded by the characters. In 1983, the third film in the series, *Star Wars: Return of the Jedi*, included even more CGI effects—some 700 images that made it into the final film were produced on the computer. For example, in the film, Luke Skywalker and Princess Leia race against Imperial Stormtroopers on gravity-defying speeder bikes that zoom through a heavily wooded forest. Most of the action for the scene was generated on a computer by animators.

George Lucas, the producer of the Star Wars movies, realized that the characters and scenarios from the films could be adapted into games. He established LucasArts, a division of his entertainment company devoted to producing games. Such games as *X-Wing*, *Rebel Assault*, and *Dark Forces* were adapted from Star Wars scenarios. Lucas also produced the films in the Indiana Jones series. Two games featuring the heroic archaeologist Indiana Jones were developed.

By the 1990s, game designers were able to provide far more graphics, speed, color, and action because of the advancements in computer technology—particularly the microprocessor, which is the tiny device in the computer that relays the user's commands to the computer, instructing the machine on what to do. Home computers had become sophisticated and were able to accept a higher degree of graphics and animation. In 1996, hardware manufacturers added a microprocessor to home machines that enabled the monitors to display graphics in three dimensions. Now players could control animated characters—seeing them from all sides and changing their viewpoints, directions, and paths through the games.

One game that shows the sophistication in animation techniques during this period debuted in 1996. The game, titled *Tomb Raider*, featured an animated main character—Lara Croft. The game designers of *Tomb Raider* strived to make the characters and scenes seem as realistic as possible, blurring the lines between real life and animation.

The purpose of the game was to retrieve ancient artifacts and battle villains along the way. In 2001, the game was adapted into a live-action movie starring Angelina Jolie as Lara Croft. This was one of the first examples of a video game being converted into a film.

Pokémon

One of the most notable examples of a video game turning into a television show is the game *Pokémon*. The game, which allowed players to catch and train animated creatures, was a big hit after becoming available to the Nintendo Game Boy in 1996. From this game stemmed a multitude of opportunities. Several other games were created to supplement the first, including games that were available on other game consoles. In 1997, the first episode of the television series aired, following a Pokémon trainer named Ash and his partner, a creature named Pikachu. The show was a huge success and allowed the franchise to remain profitable in the following years.

In 2016, a game titled *Pokémon Go* was released as an application that could be played on a smartphone. This game allows players to travel to actual locations in the real world, and, through accessing the phone's camera, catch Pokémon in real-life scenarios. The app has been a huge success and has once again made *Pokémon* one of the most popular games on the market.

What was once a console game is now a smartphone app that allows players to catch, train, and battle Pokémon in real-world settings.

Though we now see some video games that have been adapted into films and television shows, more often, we see the opposite—shows that were converted into a video game or in many cases, several different video games. Similar to the video games created after the success of the Star Wars franchise, many popular shows and films today have video games stemming from their success.

As the popularity of games increased, so did the popularity of their characters. Merchandise featuring characters from video games can be found in stores around the world and on the Internet, showing that this form of computer animation is a hit with the masses.

CHAPTER THREE

The Animation Process

Though technology has advanced an incredible amount since the early days of animation, the process of creating and completing a project is still long and tedious. Each character requires a specific range of movements and a complex means of manipulating their face and body to match those movements flawlessly. This keeps the viewer from questioning the workmanship and allows them to enjoy the experience in front of them—whether the medium is film, television, or a video game.

When animators working on the film *Monsters, Inc.*, and later, on its prequel, *Monsters University*, designed the big blue monster named Sulley, they found it necessary to employ a unique comput-er program that enabled them to move each strand of Sulley's fur—all 2.3 million of them. Creating this computer program required the talents of several software engineers. Once the program was in place, animators were able to alter each aspect of the character, allowing the character to move in a way that looked natural. In the case of *Monsters, Inc.*, this included allowing each strand of Sulley's fur to shift according to his physical movements.

Most animators working professionally today are graduates of art schools rather than computer science programs. Meanwhile, the software used to make these animations possible derives from mathematical formulas known as algorithms. Though animators are the people who create and manipulate the art that makes animation possible, software engineers play a big part in its creation. Frequently, specific software needs to be written to achieve the specific goals of a project, and animators and software engineers must work closely together to create a successful animation. At Pixar, chief creative officer John Lasseter has said his company has invested

Being able to show movements in specific details, such as Sulley's fur, allows the animator to further blur the lines between animation and real life.

heavily in technology, while keeping in mind that the artists are the ones who provide Pixar with its cinematic vision. As Lasseter explained, "Here, the art challenges the technology and the technology inspires the art."[8] Without the technological advances that have occurred throughout the history of animation, the process that makes it so successful today would not exist.

Storyboarding

When it comes to animating on the computer, artists find themselves involved early in the process. *Monsters, Inc.* as well as all other animated films—whether they are rendered on the computer or produced through cel art—begin with a concept, a script, and then a storyboard. Concepts and then scripts are typically provided by writers or the people who conceive the story, who plot out the action and compose the dialogue. After the initial concept is fleshed out, storyboarding is the next step. Drawn by artists, storyboards provide the initial visualization for how the films will look. This is a crucial part in mapping out each step for the filmmakers so that when they begin creating the film, they have a concrete vision to bring to life.

Storyboards have been used in moviemaking for decades—and not just in animated films. Essentially, an artist is called on to draw the movie, scene by scene, on large poster boards. Storyboards are often rather detailed, as their purpose is to give the director an idea of how each scene should be photographed. Working from a storyboard, a director can plot placement of cameras and sound equipment, choose the lenses for the cameras, plan how to light the scene, and decide where to stage the actors. In live-action filmmaking, storyboarding serves as a general outline. Since directors are able to see each scene acted out in real time, actors are able to move and shift to cre-ate a more accurate depiction of the initial ideas for that particular scene.

In computer animation, animators pay strict adherence to what the storyboard tells them to do, since live-action trial and error is not an option. The storyboard is very detailed because it is used to guide the animators in how to render the characters in each scene. In a film that is animated by the computer, one scene must end where the next one begins. Most animated films employ dozens or often hundreds of artists, all developing different scenes at the same time. Artists may take months to animate the scenes they have been assigned. If an artist does not strictly follow the storyboard, a choppy scene-to-scene transition may result. Therefore, a storyboard for a computer-animated movie may include thousands of images—one for each camera shot. Patrick Kriwanek, an animation professor at the University of California, Berkeley, explained the process:

> *In film, no shot exists alone; it is a sister to the incoming shot, and must flow into the next shot. It exists as part of a full-motion continuum, and it has to be pre-visualized in that way … that is why the boards for* Finding Nemo *or* Toy Story *look exactly like the boards for* Indiana Jones, *because those boards were created by filmmakers, thinking and visualizing the shots in continuity, in service of the greater flow …*

The greatest animated films of our time are great because they "feel" like a real movie, they have been constructed by filmmakers using the same guidelines we use to create powerful live-action narratives.[9]

Creating the Character

Following the storyboarding phase, the process moves into the computer. The first step in bringing a computer-animated scene to life is known as modeling. The artists who work in this phase of production are known as modelers. Typically, modelers have backgrounds in sculpture or industrial design.

A model is any three-dimensional object—most often a character—that will appear in the scene. Sometimes modeling is done by fashioning a sculpture, known as a maquette, of the character that will later be scanned into the computer. If they choose not to work from maquettes, modelers can work right on the computer, composing a character using one of two methods: polygon modeling or spline modeling.

Polygon modeling is based on a form of industrial design that was developed in 1949 by the architect R. Buckminster Fuller, who used it to design the geodesic dome. A geodesic dome is a sphere constructed by linking together the sides of triangles or similar geometric shapes, known as polygons, and angling them each slightly so they fit together to form a sphere. Modelers can fashion shapes as complicated as Sulley by building the characters through polygon construction on their computers. Generally, the first step includes scanning a sketch of the character into the computer. Next, the modeler selects points on the scanned image that will provide a general outline of the character. The computer software will then add a series of lines connecting the points. It is similar to making a sculpture out of papier-mâché; in that medium, the artist first constructs a wire skeleton on which the papier-mâché will be applied. Once a computer-animated character's skeleton has been created, the modeler can use the software to fill in the gaps with polygons. For highly detailed work that will show many curves, crevices, corners, wrinkles, bumps, hairs, and other assorted features, the polygons need to be tiny and packed closely together. This tedious process requires sophisticated computer software as well as the work of many talented modelers.

The other method of creating a character on the computer is known as splining. Campers are familiar with splines because they use them as the ribs to support domed tents. Campers first set up the splines, creating a skeleton, then stretch the tent fabric over them. As in polygon modeling, a spline modeler will first scan the drawing and then select the reference points to create the outline and skeleton of the character. Instead of filling in the gaps with polygons, the modeler will use splines. Splining can be

Maquettes help the animator to flesh out a general idea of what they want their character to look like before inputting it into the computer. Shown here is a maquette of the character Wallace from Wallace and Gromit.

accomplished with less-powerful computers than those required to produce a model with polygons, but polygons provide a more intricately detailed model. The major animation studios, with multimillion-dollar budgets at their disposal and hundreds of modelers and animators on staff, generally prefer to work with the polygon method.

Preparing Their Movements

Whether the artist works with splines or polygons, the modeler has now created a character in two dimensions. To create a three-dimensional character, other viewpoints of the character must be modeled. For a simple shape, modelers can compose three-dimensional viewpoints by working with additional sketches of the same object. For example, a modeler can compose a three-dimensional image of a bouncing ball by using sketches. This technique may not work for more complex objects or characters; in those cases, the modelers must make use of maquettes. In the large animation studios, modelers will use clay to fashion maquettes of the characters. Maquettes are generally about 14 inches (35.5 cm) tall.

The maquettes do not have to be very intricate. Later, the details of the characters' faces and bodies can be fine-tuned on the computer. The purpose of the maquette is to provide the reference points for the computer that the modeler can use to fill in with polygons or splines. After the maquette is fashioned, the modeler will typically draw a grid of black lines across its surface. Each place on the maquette where the lines of the grid intersect creates a reference point. The modeler can then use a handheld scanning device to transmit the reference points to the computer.

The computer now has in its memory every conceivable viewpoint of the figure. Whenever a viewpoint is called up on the computer monitor, the reference points are filled in with polygons or splines. At this point, the modeler may work for weeks or months refining the

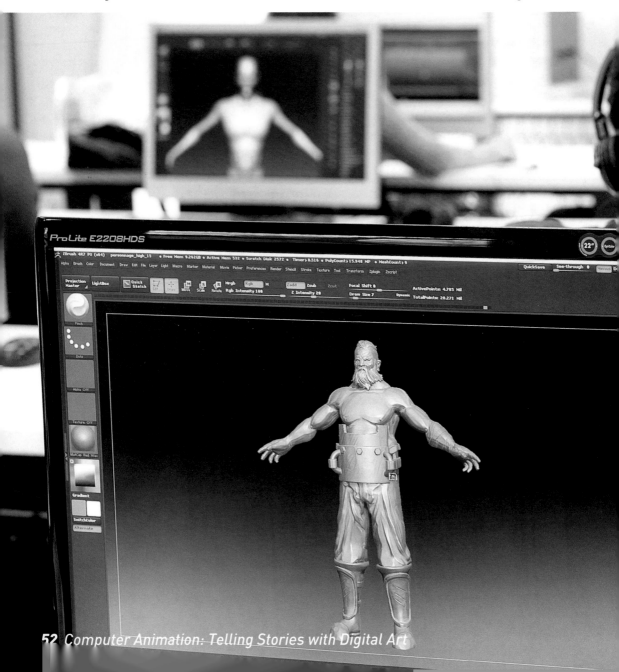

images by filling in intricate details, colors, and other features.

The character is now ready for the next step, which is known as rigging. Using the computer, the artist known as the rigger finds places on the character where the image can be manipulated to show motion. Most living things move their body at the joints in their arms, legs, neck, back, feet, hands, and other limbs. Likewise, on the computer, the rigger selects places on the character's body that will serve as joints. To select the joints, the rigger will superimpose

After creating a maquette, a skeleton can be created on the computer. This general outlay of a character can be altered to the character's movements and actions. From here, the details of the character's physical appearance can be added.

a temporary skeleton over the image of the character. When the film is shown in theaters, the audience will never see the skeleton—it will be erased long before the graphics are transferred to film—but it is vital as a tool for showing the animators where the character can bend a leg, crook a finger, or form words with his or her mouth.

According to Peter Weishar, professor of animation at New York University, rigging is one of the most important parts of animation because it governs how the character moves. As Weishar explains, how the animator designs the movements of the character is often the most vital task in convincing the audience of the authenticity of the character, "Even if the character is something as unlikely as a talking giant sloth walking upright on its hind legs, it will be believable if it seems to have weight and presence in the scene."[10] What Weishar means is that rigging the character's movements is crucial in helping the audience focus on the film, rather than any inconsistencies in the animation techniques.

To do their jobs, riggers often find studying real-life examples to be helpful. The riggers who worked on the film *Ice Age* spent a lot of time at zoos, studying the motions of big cats so that they

Making Sounds

One of the most important things to "rig" in an animation are the facial expressions of a character, more specifically, a character's mouth and lips. This job is particularly important because the lips must move in sync with the dialogue spoken in the sound studio by the actor providing the voice for the character.

To properly rig the lips, the rigger must understand how sounds are formed in the mouth. Each sound is known as a phoneme and requires different muscles in the mouth, tongue, and lips to make the sound. The sound of "m," for example, requires the lips to be pressed together. Studying how people talk is critical to accurately modeling the character's mouth movements. Therefore, the rigger must find the places in the lips and face of the character where the mouth can be moved to make the sounds seem natural. Once the lips and face are rigged, the animator runs the character through all the sounds and stores the facial expressions in the computer's memory. Then, when the spoken dialogue is added, the animator can use the appropriate facial expression to match the phoneme uttered by the actor. Riggers will also look for other places in the face that may move to accompany a sound. They may rig an eyebrow to be raised when a character uses a curious tone, curl a lip if the dialogue requires the character to be sarcastic, or cause lines to appear in the character's forehead if he or she is upset.

could properly plan the movements for Diego, the saber-toothed tiger. Weishar said, "When a tiger takes a simple step, a great deal more happens than just a leg moving forward. His tail may wag a bit, his pelvis will rotate, his back may curve, and various other parts of the body will shift to compensate for the redistribution of weight."[11] Being able to study movements of similar creatures in real life helps the riggers properly animate the movements on the computer.

Making Movements

Once the characters have been properly modeled and rigged, it is time to make them move. This is the actual animation process. Generally, teams of animators are assigned to each scene. Their job is to bring life to the characters, manipulating their motions through each scene to tell the story that has been described in the script and storyboards.

In cel animation, the characters are given motion through a series of drawings, each slightly different than the last. When the cels are run through the camera at a high rate of speed, they fool the eye into believing that the character is alive on the screen. In computer animation, there is no need to provide thousands of images of the character in slightly different poses. Instead, the animator will select a few key poses and then direct the computer in providing the motions of the characters between those poses. To accomplish this task, the animator must tell the computer how much time needs to elapse from pose to pose and which joints in the temporary skeleton must be manipulated. The computer software will then move the splines or polygons according to this information.

There is no need to produce thousands of cel drawings, but animating through the computer is still an incredibly long and tedious process. At Pixar, for example, it has taken as long as five years to animate a single film, calling on the talents of hundreds of modelers, riggers, and animators, as well as software engineers and other technical staff members. Sometimes, as in the case of manipulating Sulley's 2.3 million hairs, the engineers had to design new software simply for that one task. Weishar said, "There are thousands of details involved in every shot. Whether it is a subtle movement of the eyes, or perhaps a shift in weight that gives the character more presence in a scene, an animator can tweak a single shot for weeks."[12] In animation, a scene cannot simply be re-shot if something looks off or unnatural, since the characters are just data and images stored in a computer. An animator must perfect each movement to create a seamless transition throughout each scene, which often means that a lot of trial and error occurs in the making of a character's movements and actions.

At this point, the characters may have been modeled, rigged, and animated, but the movie is far from finished. There are many other components that must be added before the film is ready for the theaters.

Executing the Scenes

In live-action filmmaking, the sets are generally illuminated by huge lights that shine on the actors. Properly lighting a film set is a craft practiced by skilled tradespeople who must know how to make actors look natural, how to avoid projecting unflattering light, and how to create the mood the director is seeking. Since computer animation requires artificial light created through the computer, an animator must spend a lot of time making it look natural.

There is a major difference in lighting a live-action film set and lighting a computer animation. To light a film set, the lamps are positioned off set and are shone onto the actors—the lamps themselves do not appear on film, only their light. On an animation screen,

the animator cannot shine a computer-generated light onto the characters, because that light source would show up on screen. Therefore, the animator must light each character and all other components of the scene by manipulating the color and intensity of each element in the scene. It must all be coordinated so that the lighting appears to be natural. Though lighting does not seem as important as the other aspects of the film, being able to tell the difference between day and night—or even sunny days and cloudy days—is a huge part in making a film look seamless and natural.

In addition to adjusting the lighting, backgrounds must be composed for all the scenes. In traditional cel animation, an artist would paint a static

It is important for animators to differentiate the lighting in their animations. This helps the viewer distinguish whether the scene takes place during the day or at night.

scene on which the cels are placed and photographed. In computer animation, the background scenes often feature three-dimensional aspects; likewise, the viewpoints shift as the characters move through them. Still, the first step in the process of designing backgrounds requires artists to paint two-dimensional images. These images will help the computer animators design backgrounds, sticking to the concepts for the scenes that have been worked out in advance.

The final step in the process is to convert the images stored on the computer onto film, which is the only way it can be shown in theaters. In cel animation, a movie camera is aimed at the cels, which are placed in front of the lens and are filmed one frame at a time. Converting computer-animated images to film is a much more intricate process, requiring special equipment that captures the computer's digital images onto 35mm film stock. However, animators do have a role in this process. As the images are recorded on film, the animators can watch the conversion on a monitor and adjust color, light, sharpness, and other features of the images as they are transferred.

CHAPTER FOUR

Representing Real People

The processes used to create a seamless animation all strive to achieve one goal: to create an interesting storyline and to portray the scenery and characters in a way that feels both natural and entertaining. This idea is conceived in a variety of different ways. For example, in the movie *Inside Out*, the storyline follows a young girl and the feelings and thoughts that happen inside of her head, portrayed by little people that represent each emotion. The actual human characters—the girl and her family—are animated people that are meant to look, act, and move like animated people. The characters in the young girl's head, representing her emotions, are loosely based on the aspects of a person, but they have more exaggerated features and bodies composed of different colors and shapes.

There is no question that the characters are animations; even the people who are meant to portray humans look like animations and not real-life people. This is the biggest distinction between animation and computer-generated imagery—CGI is meant to trick the audience into believing that the character is real and not a 3-D-animated form.

For years, animators and filmmakers have strived to find a process that makes animation look like real life. Much like the scenes in *Star Wars: A New Hope*, animators attempt to

The comparison between the representation of characters in live-action films that use CGI and the characters in Inside Out *shows the difference between striving to create something human-like and the ability to create something that borders a more creative side.*

conceive a computer-generated scene that looks and feels like the real-life acting around it. This process, which requires the talent of many artists and engineers, took a long time to develop. Today, we see films that feature humans and creatures that are completely indistinguishable as animation. This process allows live-action films to push the boundaries of reality and enhance the storyline by creating seamless characters and scenes that don't raise questions about what is real life and what is animation.

Rotoscoping

Early cel animators attempted to create forms that looked like real people. Since cel animation was essentially a large number of drawings screened together quickly, movements of characters could seem harsh and unnatural. Today's animations are created in a way that leads each character

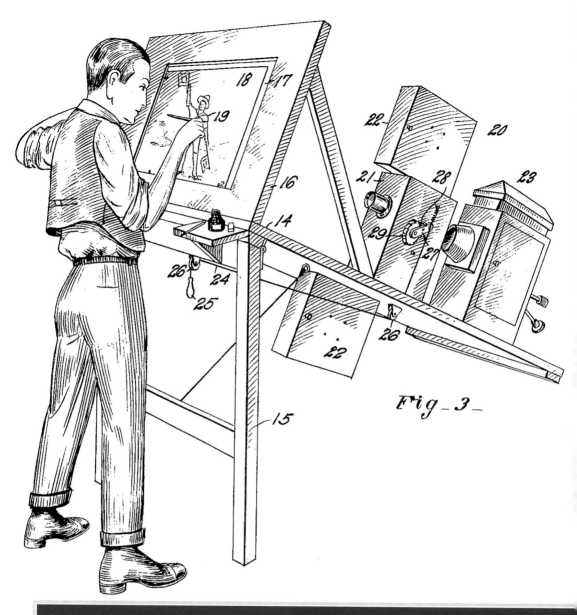

18 17
19
16
14
22 20
21 28 23
29 27
22
26
15
26 24 25

Fig-3-

Shown here is the first patent drawing of Max Fleischer's original rotoscope.

throughout the scene naturally, even if the character is a furry blue monster, such as Sulley.

There were some attempts to portray lifelike people through cel animation. The earliest attempts at this began with a process known as rotoscoping, which was a technique first used in 1914 by animator Max Fleischer. Fleischer built a projector, which he called a rotoscope, to display a series of filmed images on a screen composed of frosted white glass. Then, he traced over the images, frame by frame, to create a cartoon.

In 1937, nearly a decade after animating the first adventures of Mickey Mouse, Disney produced the film *Snow White and the Seven Dwarfs*. The producers hoped to instill a sense of realism in the film by depicting Snow White and the prince as real-life characters. In Snow White's case, dancer Marge Champion served as the model for the princess. The animators studied her on film and copied her movements into drawings. Cel animators continued trying different variations of these studies to help their characters look more lifelike. Following the success of *Snow White and the Seven Dwarfs*, Disney released *Cinderella* in 1950, *Alice in Wonderland* in 1951, and *Sleeping Beauty* in 1959; in each case, some of the humans were drawn to look human, although there is no question that in each film, some of the other characters were drawn as caricatures, not representative of a real person. Martin Goodman said, "Disney's films continued to feature human protagonists and typically did not falter in doing so. As realism and naturalism became desirable goals, the human figure was a proving ground for animators."[13] Nevertheless, as well crafted as *Cinderella*, *Alice in Wonderland*, and *Sleeping Beauty* may have been, no animator working on any of those films had the slightest doubt that the audience would fail to see *Cinderella*, *Alice in Wonderland*, and *Sleeping Beauty* for what they were— cartoon drawings.

Motion Capture

One of the most common and effective ways to achieve the look of a real person in animation is through a process called motion capture. To perform motion capture, an actor wears a suit containing hundreds of reflective sensors, which are mostly sewn into the joints but also appear elsewhere on the costume. As the actor moves, the camera reads the light reflected by the sensors, thus making a digital record of the actor's motions and turning them into a sort of skeleton. More broadly, this process is referred to as performance capture, since the person wearing the suit must act out each movement the animated character will need to make. This process also includes the capturing of facial expressions. After the actor performs each movement in a scene, the information is transferred to the computer, allowing the animator to paint over the skeleton with the art for the character.

The 2002 film *The Lord of the Rings: The Two Towers* made extensive use of motion capture to animate the character of Gollum, a corrupted hobbit who leads Frodo on his quest to destroy the powerful One Ring. Gollum was a CGI character, but he was animated through the use of motion capture. The filmmakers dressed actor Andy Serkis in a motion-capture suit and had him portray Gollum in all the scenes. Then, the filmmakers used motion capture to animate Gollum,

Using motion capture to create movements for an animated character is one of the most effective ways for an animation to reflect natural movements and features.

matching his motions up perfectly to those made by Serkis. Finally, Gollum was digitally inserted into the movie's scenes accordingly.

Facial recognition software is used for motion capture as well. The movie *Avatar*, which broke the boundaries between live acting and animation, used facial expression motion capture to hone in on the feelings of the animated characters. This film follows its main character, Jake, to another world where all of its inhabitants are blue, alien-like creatures. Live acting is used for the scenes where Jake is portrayed in the real world, wherein animation is used for the creatures on Pandora. For this animation to be achieved, 52 small,

01:00:45.29

ND 08:56:18:11. ST.

SC26A -AA6 , TK09

green sensors were placed on the faces of the actors. Tiny cameras were held directly in front of their faces to capture each muscle movement. The actors then played out the scenes with each other. Since the sensors translated to the computer so quickly, the production team was able to film the characters around the virtual scene on their computer.

Using motion capture techniques for The Polar Express *allowed the noticeably animated characters to still look human.*

Animation and *The Polar Express*

Although *The Lord of the Rings: The Two Towers* and the other films in the Lord of the Rings and the Hobbit series are full of CGI effects, the films are still essentially live-action movies. In 2004, Castle Rock Entertainment released *The Polar Express*, a computer-animated film made entirely through the motion-capture process. The film, based on a children's book written in 1985 by author and illustrator Chris Van Allsburg, tells the story of a young boy who loses his faith in Santa Claus. On Christmas Eve, a magical train called the Polar Express appears at the boy's home and whisks him to the North Pole, where he meets Santa Claus. At the North Pole, the boy finds a huge mechanized factory, rather than a quaint storybook workshop where elves make toys by hand. When the boy arrives, Santa selects him to receive the first gift of Christmas—a bright silver bell from Santa's sleigh. To make the film, director Robert Zemeckis elected to use the process of motion capture to animate all the characters.

Six of the characters, including the train's conductor and Santa Claus, were portrayed by Tom Hanks, who donned the motion-capture suit and performed all six roles in front of a blank screen. Zemeckis pointed out that acting a role in a motion capture suit can be far more difficult than playing a role on the stage

CGI and *Fantastic Beasts*

Another movie in the Harry Potter wizarding world hit theaters in November 2016. The film *Fantastic Beasts and Where to Find Them* follows a wizard named Newt Scamander through New York City in 1926, as he collects and cares for magical creatures. This film, created by many of the same artists as the Harry Potter films, exudes the same quality of CGI as the previous films, except this storyline called for much more than just a handful of full CGI creatures. Hundreds of creatures were drawn out before production, each with many different variations. They employed many highly skilled artists to create maquettes and puppets of the creatures so the cast could act alongside them. Tim Burke, the visual effects supervisor for *Fantastic Beasts* as well as each Harry Potter film, described the making of the creatures:

Creature design always serves a purpose. Before [the **Harry Potter** *series], we'd scan a maquette and try to fix the creature in post. But now, because we were creating it and animating it, we knew what it was. All the creatures had character. That helped everyone.*[1]

Creating both an animated and physical mock-up of the creatures allowed production to give each one a personality, making it both look and feel real to the viewers.

1. Quoted in Barbara Robertson, "Magical By Design," *Computer Graphics World*, Volume: 39, Issue: 6, November/December 2016. www.cgw.com/Publications/CGW/2016/Volume-39-Issue-6-Nov-Dec-2016-/Magical-by-Design.aspx.

in front of an audience. For example, when the part requires the actor to handle a prop, the actor has to go through the motions required in the script without the actual prop in his or her hands. "I believe the only thing Tom missed was having the physical trappings of a costume," Zemeckis said. "He had to remember that the conductor wore glasses when he was the conductor and he had to remember to touch the bill of his cap or adjust his collar, which he would have done more instinctively if he had been actually wearing that wardrobe."[14]

Of course, the animators had a lot more work to do than just create and animate characters based on the movements of Hanks and the other actors. They had to concoct a whole universe of landscapes, backgrounds, and other features for the film that had to appear as real as if they were filmed for a live-action production. Zemeckis also insisted that the look of the film be based on the illustrations Van Allsburg

In the film Fantastic Beasts and Where to Find Them, *at least 200 different variations of the character Pickett, a small, green, plant-like creature, were mocked up. Actors used maquettes during filming to allow their motions and interactions with the animations to look natural.*

painted for the book. Thus, before the first drawings were made for the film, the production company's artists traveled to Van Allsburg's boyhood home in Grand Rapids, Michigan, where they made sketches of the home and neighborhood, which they intended to use for the backgrounds in the film.

Even the costumes worn by the animated characters received special attention by the filmmakers. Ordinarily, the animators may be left on their own to concoct the costumes for the animated characters, but in this case, the filmmakers called in a Hollywood costume designer, who designed the costumes and then had them sewn and fitted to the actors. Of course, the actors did not wear the costumes during the motion-capture sequences. Instead, the costumes were scanned and their images were downloaded into the computers. They were modeled and rigged and placed on the animated characters, allowing them to flow and move naturally, just as they would on a real person.

Production of *The Polar Express* turned out to be a complicated and expensive undertaking. It took 4 years and an investment of $170 million to bring the 100-minute movie to the screen. Most film critics applauded the quality of the computer animation, but they also suggested that the filmmakers fell short of producing convincing depictions of humans. Though they did not resemble real humans, film critic Roger Ebert still found the characters endearing. He said, "The characters in *The Polar Express* don't look real, but they don't look unreal, either; they have a simplified and underlined reality that makes them visually magnetic."[15]

CGI and Harry Potter

Though the animation style of *The Polar Express* did not achieve the look of real humans, breakthroughs in film were beginning to do so both with and without modern motion-capture techniques. Another character, similar to Gollum from *Lord of the Rings*, fooled viewers into second-guessing its authenticity. This character is from the Harry Potter series written by J.K. Rowling, which was then adapted into a movie series. This story follows Harry Potter and his quest to defeat Voldemort. The Harry Potter film franchise was—and still is—one of the most profitable in the world. Many scenes in each of the films—even the earliest ones—represent some of the most impeccable CGI work seen today. One of the most notable examples first appeared in the second film adaptation, *Harry Potter and the Chamber of Secrets*. Dobby, an enslaved house elf, appears in the film for the first time as he warns Harry Potter of the dangers of returning to Hogwarts School of Witchcraft and Wizardry. Dobby's character is a small creature that is both bold and nervous. The most impressive characteristic of Dobby, however, was that he looked real, but was created entirely through computer animation.

George Lucas' animation firm, Industrial Light and Magic, created the

A new way of shading skin was created for Dobby's character. This shading software allowed his skin to reflect light in a very natural way, further adding to his realistic features.

character for the film. Unlike Gollum, Dobby was not created using motion capture but instead was rendered entirely on the computer. The actor playing Harry, Daniel Radcliffe, acted the scenes with the house elf using a ball on a stick for reference. Dave Adams, the animation director of the film, said in an interview for *Computer Graphics World*, "He's photoreal, he's acting alongside Daniel Radcliffe, who plays Harry, and he exhibits the subtlety of a real actor. He's the new bar at ILM (Industrial Light and Magic) against which future characteristics will be compared."[16] Several different aspects came together to create such a memorable character. Software programs were created to achieve his lifelike skin, as well as lighting techniques that helped the creature appear convincing in a real-world setting.

CHAPTER FIVE

Future Opportunities

Computer animation techniques have come a long way since their beginnings, and the range of opportunities this field has is growing every day. Due to technological advances, computer-animated films, games, and television shows have dominated the entertainment industry for many years and will continue to do so. Films now feature characters that are completely indistinguishable as animation. These processes continue to advance and shape the uses for and ideas behind computer animation. Animation, however entertaining, breaks the boundaries of just being functional for entertainment purposes, allowing computer animation techniques to be used in different aspects of everyday life. Now that people know how to manipulate something into a 3-D form or sequence, other opportunities for this medium have been identified.

Animation in films has reached a point where live actors and animated characters can be interchangeable in some cases. Because of this, computer-animated movies are among the most profitable films each year in the box office. The gaming industry continues to create thought-provoking games that provide hours of decision-making through scenarios with characters that appear real. Furthering these advancements has taken significant amounts of time and creativity over the years. However, animation now also serves a purpose beyond entertainment. Medical professionals are now able to look at detailed 3-D renderings of body parts to help further their learning on specific topics. Architects and designers now have the opportunity to flesh out a project through animation before beginning construction. Virtual reality headsets are available that allow a player's physical movements to alter a game or, in some instances, make them feel as if they are in actual, real-world places by providing a 360-degree viewpoint. Marketing techniques use animation to captivate consumers and to further explain the use and purpose of a product or service. Animation is a part of so many aspects of the world, and its applications continue to expand each day.

Animation in Marketing

Marketing teams use animation in almost all aspects of product and service advertising. From television commercials to online marketing videos, animation is a key aspect in both gaining the attention of a consumer, as well as accurately describing the product to

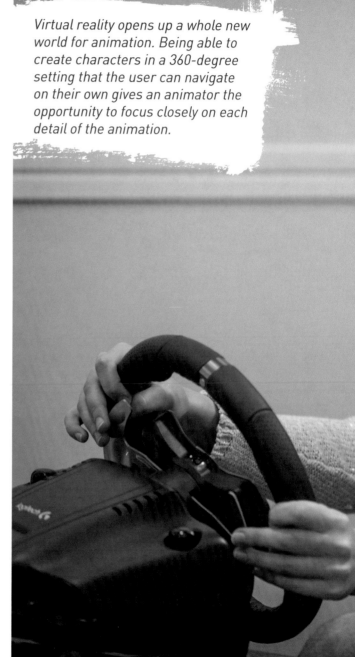

Virtual reality opens up a whole new world for animation. Being able to create characters in a 360-degree setting that the user can navigate on their own gives an animator the opportunity to focus closely on each detail of the animation.

the viewer. Something as simple as having a good marketing angle can make a company millions of dollars. However, in the case of having a not-so-great marketing angle, this can cost the company sales and give it a bad reputation. In the past, and more commonly today, brands have created a quirky spokesperson for their product who is featured in commercials and ads targeting a specific audience. A common animated character in commercial marketing techniques is the GEICO Gecko. Others include the M&M's characters, the Pillsbury Doughboy, and Mr. Peanut.

Another example of successful marketing using animation comes from the world of technology. Apple is a very popular brand. Founded by the late Steve Jobs, it is no surprise that this tech company dominates sales and consumer ratings through its successful marketing techniques. These techniques often include descriptive animated videos on each product, giving the consumer the ability to walk step-by-step through the design, functionality, and purpose of a new product.

One of its more recent video advertising campaigns, which features Apple's new health application, has proved to be well-received among consumers. This set of simple, educational videos features a mix of real-world shots of ordinary items, such as bikes and fruit, that seamlessly blend into animated segments of similar images.

The purpose of the video is to show the importance of monitoring health

and the ways in which Apple's app can help consumers achieve their goals. It achieves this in a memorable way through the use of animation.

Apple has consistently achieved success with its advertising campaigns while incorporating computer animation elements into ads.

Animation techniques such as this one play a crucial role in creating marketing material that is captivating enough to get people interested in a brand and its products.

Architects, Doctors, and Lawyers

Architects and interior designers use computer animation to provide virtual tours for their clients, showing them how their new homes will look, inside and out, from various angles and points of view. In contrast to looking at a blueprint, these animations can essentially walk a person step-by-step through a new building or home, providing the option to choose between specific architectural choices and showing how the structure will come together as a whole. As new construction is often expensive and time-consuming, being able to take a virtual walk-through of the home or building proves to be helpful. Modeling an animated home for a client is essentially no different than modeling a scene in a movie. When architects design a project for a client, they often do not have to start from scratch. They may have already stored images of walls, doors, windows, furniture, trees, and other features into their computers' memories. For example, instead of modeling a new door for every room in the house, they can simply drop the images into the animation wherever the plans call for a door, adjusting visual properties as needed.

Large architectural and design firms may employ their own animators. For small, simple projects, some architects and designers may be able to build the animation on their own using hardware and software specifically designed for modest animations. For something

more complicated, many architectural and design firms are likely to retain the services of animation studios that specialize in providing architectural animations. "We've found that it takes a

Shown here is a 3-D rendering an interior designer would produce to plan the layout of a modern living room.

team of people to do what we're doing," said Joseph Bayer, president of an Ohio-based animation studio that specializes in architectural work. "We have someone who models, someone who does the actual texturing, lighting and animation paths, and someone else who does the video editing."[17] Being able to create an animation of a home or project before construction begins allows the architect to look through the structure to make adjustments and to fix any problems that may arise during construction. It also gives the people commissioning the building a chance to request changes or propose new ideas before the structure is even started.

In addition to architects and designers, other professionals who can make use of computer animation are physicians and medical students. Several animation studios now specialize in providing animated views of human anatomy, as well as animated run-throughs of surgical procedures. These 3-D animations give students the opportunity to not only become familiar with each organ and body part inside and out, but also help them recognize the effects diseases have on organs such as the heart, lungs, and liver. Surgeons faced with difficult operations have made use of animated run-throughs, helping them decide which techniques to employ when they actually cut into their patients, as well as which problems might arise during the procedure. Pharmaceutical companies have commissioned animations to show how their drugs affect areas of the body.

Hybrid Medical Animations, a medical animation studio based out of Minneapolis, Minnesota, provides medical professionals with animations that give in-depth, and often interactive, 3-D views of specific organs and bodily processes. In 2015, they created a 3-D interactive animation of each part

Medical professionals can benefit greatly from the use of animation. For example, having the opportunity to look vitually at each part of an eye helps in both understanding how it functions as well as understanding how to fix any problems with it.

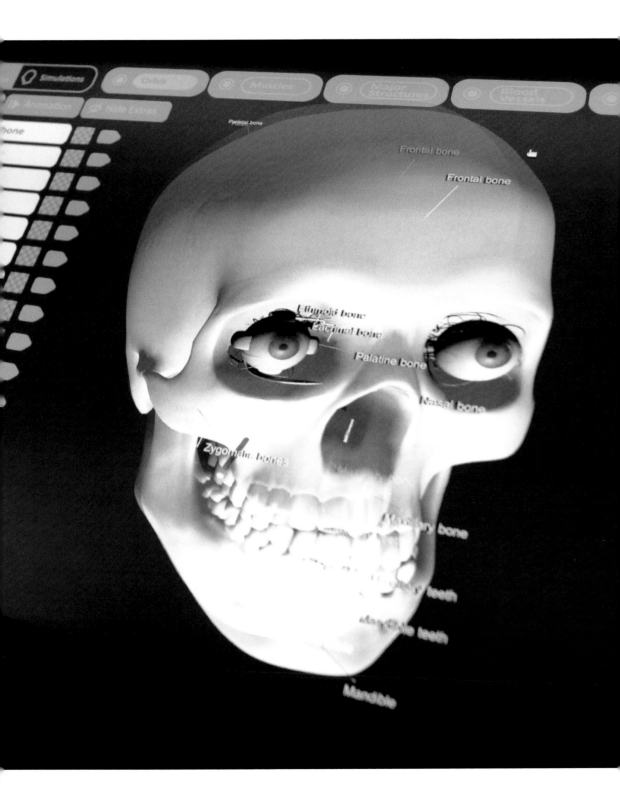

of the brain. The animation moves as the student or professional clicks around it, offering different options to further inspect the inside chambers of the brain. Since being able to sift through each part of the brain is something that is not readily available to students, being able to click through an animation that represents an exact replica is an incredible tool to help students and practicing professionals get a clear understanding of the organ. This company has also ventured into using virtual reality as a tool to further their animations. Students are now able to see 360-degree views of internal organs and ways they are altered, giving them a front-row seat to each process as the animation progresses through the body.

Doctors, physical therapists, and sports trainers have made use of motion-capture technology to determine whether patients recovering from injuries were slowing their recoveries because of the way they walk, run, or use their limbs. This tool is also used by athletes to determine how to adjust their skills to better achieve their goals or prevent injuries. One place where motion-capture technology has been used to study sports injuries is Boise State University, which has established a computer animation studio across the street from the school's football stadium.

Athletes who participate in the program wear motion-capture sensors on their bodies and are filmed running on a treadmill and performing other exercises by six cameras that record light reflected by the sensors. Animators then build models of the athletes in their computers, using their body motions as guides—similar to how Tom Hanks was animated in *The Polar Express*.

By studying the animations, the Boise State researchers can tell whether a foot injury may be aggravated by the way an athlete lands on the balls of his or her feet or whether pitchers or quarterbacks may be aggravating their shoulder injuries by the way they throw. "There's still a lot we don't know about the factors that contribute to sports injuries," said Michelle Sabick, a biomedical researcher at Boise State. "It's a fascinating field of study."[18]

The Boise State researchers are also using motion-capture animation for more than just diagnosing sports injuries. Animation provides doctors and researchers a means of being able to hone in on a specific action or skill and analyze ways that the player can improve upon it, such as a golf swing. Another service that Boise State offers is using animation techniques to perfectly fit a bike to a person's body so that they can adjust each specific part to match their body and riding techniques. As the technology behind animation expands, its applications in sports medicine and the way it can improve both an injury and a skill are expanding.

Using motion capture also allows physicians to analyze a patient after a major health problem, such as a stroke. By capturing a patient's movements and transferring them into animations

Athletes use motion-capture technology to prevent and monitor injuries, as well as to improve their skill and performance.

on a computer for study, doctors are able to compare and contrast ways in which their mobility can be improved. Through studying the movements of a healthy, fully mobile person, doctors are able to track specific joint movements and progress in the stroke patient, helping to find ways in which they can further extend their rehabilitation.

In sports medicine, animation is used as an investigative tool, allowing medical professionals to further research a topic or condition in order

Sometimes legal professionals even use computer animations to provide simulations to take a courtroom back to the scene of a crime.

to find ways to better treat it. Attorneys have found that computer animation can be used as an investigative tool as well. They have employed it to simulate car collisions in cases where one or both parties involved are being sued. The animated simulations show all the important details of the accident, including a depiction of the scene, the weather conditions, the directions the cars were traveling, and other factors that may have caused the collision. Animators take the data provided to them by witnesses and court records and create a brief movie that juries can view to determine guilt and fix monetary damages. Several cases have been won due to a convincing animation that proves the other person guilty.

Virtual Reality Takes Over

Though the history of animation has progressed drastically over the years, the vehicles through which animations are presented have changed as well. Another breakthrough in animation is the use of virtual reality headsets. These headsets allow the user to control a game or setting using their own actions, while viewing the game or film through a headpiece that covers their face, allowing them to only see the screen in front of them. The idea behind virtual reality headsets is to seamlessly merge the experience with the technology, making the viewer feel like they are part of the animated world in front of them. As the player moves, their headset tracks those movements and moves the animation along with their motions. Since gaming and film are primarily focused on the scene in front of the player, allowing a full range of motion opens up a whole new realm of possibilities to animators.

Creating an experience wherein the viewer is able to view the entire conceived scene, not just the viewpoint in front of them, allows animators to create an entire animated world in 360-degree view. As the viewer turns, the scene turns, as if they were standing in the middle of it. Virtual reality films have become popular over the past few years. One film in particular, titled *Henry*, won an Emmy award in September of 2016. This animated tale featuring a hedgehog that throws itself a birthday party was created by one of the top virtual reality companies, Oculus. The company employed a separate division, Story Studio, which is devoted to creating virtual reality films. Several well-known animators, many who have contributed to the production of the top animated movies, created *Henry*. The first scene of the film shows Henry's home. Viewers standing with the virtual headset on are able to physically walk around, exploring each detail of the tiny hedgehog's home, including being able to lean in and get a closer look at things. Ramiro Lopez Dau, the director of *Henry* and an animator on the movie *Monsters University*, said in an interview with the *Los Angeles*

Times, "What feels normal in traditional film feels fast here, and what feels boring in traditional film feels good here … In VR [virtual reality], we're learning that you don't need a character to do as much to be interesting."[19] Being able to physically move through an animated space allows the viewer to focus more on the details of the setting and characters, honing in on small details of the

film that would be otherwise impossible to see in normal films. Animators who create virtual reality films must take extra care to meticulously execute a character or scene, since it is up to the viewer how long and how closely they want to spend on a specific detail.

Viewers of the virtual reality film Henry are able to move around the hedgehog's home and examine it in detail. As the viewer turns around, the scene moves with them; if they lean in closer, the scene zooms in naturally, allowing for a closer look.

Bringing Back the Dead

One of the most interesting break-throughs in animation occurred in the Star Wars film called *Rogue One: A Star Wars Story*. The film touched upon scenes and characters from the first Star Wars film, released in 1977, because it took place right before the events of that first film. The directors decided that some scenes required the use of previous characters from past films to further connect the storylines. One character in particular is Grand Moff Tarkin, known as the commander of the Death Star. The actor who played him, Peter Cushing, passed away in 1994. The filmmakers were faced with a decision: explain why the commander of the Death Star was not a part of a scene that specifically involves him, cast a different actor, or attempt to create an animation using Cushing's previous shots from the first film and employ them in the scene. They chose the last option. Employees of Industrial Light and Magic began to conquer the task.

They hired an actor of similar features and stature and then had him act out each necessary scene in a motion capture outfit. From there, they uploaded everything onto a computer and began the process of what creative officer John Knoll referred to as "a super high-tech and labor-intensive ver-

Being able to digitally paint a person's face onto another actor's body through motion capture allows films to not only bring back deceased actors, but to refer back to earlier films where the actors are younger and look a lot different.

sion of doing makeup."[20] Using scenes that Cushing had acted out in previous films, the creators were essentially able to digitally paint his face onto the actor's body for each scene. Several aspects of this process proved difficult; factors such as lighting and the stand-in actor's mouth movements differed from the original footage. The team, however, succeeded in creating believable scenes with the commander of the Death Star, seemingly placing an actor who had long since passed into new footage. The end of the film uses this technique a second time, when a young Princess Leia, played by the late Carrie Fisher,

returns at the end of the film for a brief scene.

The studio has stated that this technique is not one they plan to use often, since the process is time-consuming, difficult, and expensive. The option that it poses, however, opens up a huge variety of opportunities for live-action CGI films in the future.

Future Animators

Becoming skilled in computer animation takes many years of perfecting multiple skills. Though there are many different types of animators, each one shares the same fundamental skills. One of the most important skills needed to

become a skilled animator is drawing. It is important to understand how people, animals, and objects are constructed to be able to make them move on a computer. Understanding how to translate those movements into 2-D and 3-D drawings is a crucial first step in animation. Another important skill is understanding the computer programs used to create an animation. Many different software programs are required to successfully execute an animation, and understanding how to efficiently and accurately navigate through them is an important skill. Ringling College of Art and Design in Florida offers one of the top animation programs in the United States. Aside from several animation-based classes, the curriculum for their four-year program includes drawing and figure drawing classes, as well as classes in 2-D and 3-D design. Many colleges around the country offer excellent programs in computer animation, some more specifically geared toward a particular skill within the title, such as medical and forensic animation. If someone decides to pursue a career in computer animation, finding a good college to help them perfect their knowledge and skills is important.

To become skilled at computer animation, one must know how to draw everyday objects for them to look realistic when transferred to a computer.

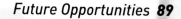

Some high school art departments even offer introductory courses in computer animation. One school that has taken the lead in training future computer animators is Penn Manor High School in Lancaster, Pennsylvania, where 275 students a year take classes in computer animation, digital photography, and web design.

Students who enroll in the animation class write scripts, provide the sketches for their characters, record the voices, and model the characters on the school's computers. By the end of the course, most of the computer animators create short movies that span a few minutes. Penn Manor's program is regarded as one of the top high school computer animation programs in the country. Teacher Shawn Canady said, "You watch students come in with a limited ability to represent themselves digitally; and then they (are able to) create amazing graphics—visually rich representations of their imagination."[21] Studying animation can be an interesting and rewarding career path, but a large amount of practice and dedication goes into perfecting the skill. Top animators throughout the industry's history worked and studied hard to achieve the progress in animation that is seen today.

The history of animation has progressed such a great deal that there is no telling where it will lead in the future. The industry has come a long way since the beginnings of cel animation in filmmaking. Today's ani-

There are many computer animation programs offered at the collegiate level. Some high schools even offer introductory courses in the subject.

mations are sometimes completely indistinguishable from real people, and remakes of old cel animation films using computer animation can offer audiences a different perspective on a familiar story from a technologically new standpoint. Animation is everywhere, providing entertainment and selling new products. Its evolution has advanced rapidly, and new techniques and practices are developed every day. Though the future of animation is unknown, if it follows in the footsteps of its history, there are many exciting things to come.

Notes

Introduction:
The Beginning of Animation

1. Brent Schlender, "Interview with Steve Jobs," *Fortune*, September 18, 1995. archive.fortune.com/ magazines/fortune/fortune_ archive/1995/09/18/206099/ index.htm.

Chapter One:
Progression
of Techniques

2. Charles Solomon, *Enchanted Drawings: The History of Animation*. New York, NY: Wings, 1994, p. 40.
3. Quoted in Paul Trachtman, "Charles Csuri Is an 'Old Master' in a NewMedium," *Smithsonian Magazine*, February 1995, p. 56.

4. Quoted in Joe Tracy, "An Inside Look at the Original Beauty and the Beast," *Digital Media FX Magazine*. www. digitalmediafx.com/Beauty/ Features/originalbeauty.html.

Chapter Two:
The Gaming Industry

5. Keith Ferrell, "Quiet on the Set: Interaction!," *Omni*, November 1991, p. 93.
6. Quoted in B.I. Koerner, "How Pong Invented Geekdom," *U.S. News & World Report*, December 27, 1999, p. 67.
7. Quoted in David Sheff, *Game Over: How Nintendo Zapped an American Industry, Captured Your Dollars, and Enslaved Your Children*. New York, NY: Random House, 1993, p. 136.

Chapter Three: The Animation Process

8. Quoted in John Horn, "Enough Pixels, Time for Comedy Class," *Newsweek*, April 29, 2002, p. 46.
9. Patrick Kriwanek, "Storytelling Through Cuts," *Animation Mentor Report*, October 2005. www.animationmentor.com/ newsletter.1005/feature_ storytelling.html.
10. Peter Weishar, *Blue Sky: The Art of Computer Animation*. New York, NY: Harry N. Abrams, 2002, p. 28.
11. Weishar, *Blue Sky*, p. 29.
12. Weishar, *Blue Sky*, p. 67.

Chapter Four: Representing Real People

13. Martin Goodman, "Dr. Toon: Running with the Pack," *AnimationWorld*, November 15, 2006. mag.awn.com/?article_ no=3081.
14. Quoted in Julian Phillips, "Performance Capture CGI Techniques Makes 'The Polar Express' an Advance for Animation," *Skwigly Animation Magazine*, October 27, 2004. www.skwigly.co.uk/ magazine/news/article. asp?articleid=346&zoneid=3.
15. Roger Ebert, "The Polar Express," *Chicago Sun-Times*, November 10, 2004. www.rogerebert.suntimes. com/apps/pbcs.dll/ article?AID=/20041109/ REVIEWS/41006005.
16. Audrey Doyle, "Pivotal Role," *Computer Graphics World*. Volume: 26 Issue: 2, February 2003. www.cgw.com/Publications/ CGW/2003/Volume-26-Issue-2-Feb-2003-/Pivotal-Role.aspx.

Chapter Five: Future Opportunities

17. Diana Phillips Mahoney, "Moving Beyond CAD," *Computer Graphics World*, June 1997, p. 20.
18. Quoted in *Idaho Statesman*, "BSU Professor Studies Sports Injuries," December 17, 2006.
19. Steven Zeitchik, "With 'Henry,' a Cinematic Leap into World of Virtual Reality," *Los Angeles Times*, July 28, 2015. www. latimes.com/entertainment/ movies/la-et-mn-oculus-vr-henry-20150728-story.html.
20. David Itzkoff, "How 'Rogue One' Brought Back Familiar Faces," *New York Times*, December 27, 2016. www. nytimes.com/2016/12/27/ movies/how-rogue-one-brought-back-grand-moff-tarkin.html?_r=1.

21. Quoted in Robyn Meadows, "Making Cutting-Edge Animation; Capitalizing on Teens' Growing Interest in Technology, Video Games, and Art, Penn Manor Begins Offering Computer Animation Classes," Lancaster Online, November 23, 2004. lancasteronline.com/news/making-cutting-edge-animation/article_936a7abf-2a50-51ba-93e0-53a6301b20ce.html.

For More Information

Books:

Gilbert, Sara. *The Story of Pixar*. Mankato, MN: Creative Education, 2015.
    This book provides a look at the history and accomplishments of the Pixar movie studio.

Owen, Ruth, and Ian Failes. *Creating Visual Effects for Movies as a CGI Artist*. New York, NY: Ruby Tuesday Books, Ltd., 2017.
    This book is an introduction to how CGI characters are created with fun activities for the reader.

Rauf, Don. *Getting Paid to Work in 3D*. New York, NY: Rosen Publishing, 2017.
    This book provides a look into how three-dimensional technology works in movies, gaming, apps, and social media.

Roberts, Laura. *Careers in Gaming*. San Diego, CA: ReferencePoint Press, Inc., 2017.
    This book provides an overview of what it takes to become a game designer, including updated information from people working in the industry, as well as current practices and processes.

Small, Cathleen. *Computer Animation*. New York, NY: Cavendish Square, 2015.
    This book gives readers information about careers in computer animation, including the skills and education needed, as well as expected salaries.

Websites:

Animation World Network

www.awn.com

Animation World has interviews and articles about top animation projects, as well as information about the latest technology in the animation industry.

Computer Graphics World

www.cgw.com

This website offers a wide range of information on computer animation, including blogs of practicing animators, interviews with famous pioneers of the craft, and up-to-date information on current films and games in the industry.

Disney Movies

movies.disney.com

This website provides a look into movies created by Disney, as well as blogs and articles about Disney-specific projects.

Industrial Light and Magic

www.ilm.com

The website of Industrial Light and Magic's studio provides examples of past and current projects. It also provides links to articles pertaining to CGI special effects that give a more in-depth look into the process.

Pixar

www.pixar.com

Pixar's website gives a comprehensive history of the company and its acquisition by Disney. It also provides an updated library of films created by the studio.

Index

Picture Credits

Cover Dikiiy/Shutterstock.com; pp. 1, 3–4, 6, 11, 31, 45, 59, 71, 93, 96, 98, 103–104 Lunarus/Shutterstock.com; p. 7 Earl Theisen/Getty Images; pp. 8–9, pp. 64–65 AF archive/Alamy Stock Photo; pp. 8, 16, 23, 27–28, 33–34, 43, 46, 51, 53, 57, 65, 68, 72, 78, 85, 87, 90 (caption background) Jaroslav Machacek/Shutterstock.com; pp. 12–13 Le thaumatrope : en 1825 John Ayrton Paris/Bridgeman Images; p. 15 Anne Cusack/Los Angeles Times via Getty Images; pp. 16–17 Entertainment Pictures/Alamy Stock Photo; pp. 22–23 ScreenProd/Photononstop/Alamy Stock Photo; p. 26 Pictorial Press Ltd/Alamy Stock Photo; pp. 27, 63 Photo 12/Alamy Stock Photo; pp. 28–29 Sarunyu L/Shutterstock.com; pp. 32–33 Waldir/Wikimedia Commons; pp. 34–35 Adolph/ullstein bild via Getty Images; p. 39 AAron Ontiveroz/The Denver Post via Getty Images; p. 40 julie deshaies/Shutterstock.com; p. 42 Matthew Corley/Shutterstock.com; p. 43 Marc Bruxelle/Shutterstock.com; pp. 46–47 United Archives GmbH/Alamy Stock Photo; pp. 50–51 In Pictures Ltd./Corbis via Getty Images; pp. 52–53 Andia/UIG via Getty Images; pp. 56–57 Atlaspix/Alamy Stock Photo; p. 60 © Walt Disney Studios Motion Pictures/courtesy Everett Collection; p. 61 McZusatz/Wikimedia Commons; p. 67 © Warner Bros./courtesy Everett Collection; pp. 68–69 neftali/Shutterstock.com; pp. 72–73 Alexandru Nika/Shutterstock.com; pp. 74–75 View Apart/Shutterstock.com; pp. 76–77 Robert Kneschke/Shutterstock.com; pp. 78–79 JEAN-FRANCOIS MONIER/AFP/Getty Images; p. 81 Loren Orr/Getty Images; p. 82 everything possible/Shutterstock.com; pp. 84–85 AP Photo/Eric Risberg; pp. 86–87 Sunset Boulevard/Corbis via Getty Images; pp. 88–89 Africa Studio/Shutterstock.com; pp. 90–91 Mediaphotos/Shutterstock.com; back cover vector illustration/Shutterstock.com.

About the Author

Tanya Dellaccio graduated from Fredonia College, where she received her Bachelor of Arts degree in both English and graphic design. She currently resides in Buffalo, New York, where she is both a writer and a designer.